SOMATIC EXPERIENCING THERAPY

Unlocking Healing Potential, A Comprehensive Guide To Trauma Recovery, Stress Relief, Emotional Resilience, Techniques, Practices, And Strategies For Overcoming Anxiety

COYNE LUCERO

© [2024], [COYNE LUCERO]

All rights reserved.

No part of this publication may be reproduced, distributed, or transmitted in any form or by any means, including photocopying, recording, or other electronic or mechanical methods, without the prior written permission of the publisher, except in the case of brief quotations embodied in critical reviews and certain other noncommercial uses permitted by copyright law.

DISCLAIMER

This book is intended to provide general information and guidance on various aspects of therapy and mental health. The author has made every effort to ensure that the information presented in this book is accurate and up-to-date at the time of publication.

However, the author makes no representations or warranties of any kind, express or implied, about the completeness, accuracy, reliability, suitability, or availability of the information contained herein.

The information provided in this book is for educational and informational purposes only and is not intended as a substitute for professional advice, diagnosis, or treatment. Readers are encouraged to consult with qualified mental health professionals or medical professionals for diagnosis and treatment of any mental health or medical conditions.

The author disclaims any liability for any loss or damage arising from reliance on the information provided in this book.

The views expressed in this book are solely those of the author and do not necessarily reflect the views of any organization, institution, company, business, or individual. The author is not affiliated with any company, business, or individual mentioned in this book, unless explicitly stated otherwise.

This book is based on the author's knowledge, understanding, and experience in the field of therapy and mental health. While every effort has been made to ensure the accuracy and reliability of the information presented, readers are advised to use their discretion and judgment in applying the information to their individual circumstances.

By reading this book, readers agree to indemnify and hold harmless the author from any and all claims, damages, losses, or liabilities arising from their use of or reliance on the information presented herein.

Table of Contents

ABOUT THIS BOOK

"Somatic Experiencing Therapy" is more than just another trauma resolution book; it's a thorough guide that digs into the delicate relationship between the mind and body in the healing process after traumatic situations. From its fundamental concepts to practical strategies and real-life case studies, this book provides vital insights for therapists and people wanting to understand and overcome trauma.

The first chapter introduces readers to the idea of Somatic Experiencing Therapy, discussing its origins, growth, and core understanding of the mind-body relationship. Understanding the physiology of trauma, as detailed in Chapter 2, gives critical insights into how trauma impacts the body on a neurobiological level, offering light on the processes that underpin traumatic experiences.

Chapters 3 and 4 are crucial to the book since they describe the foundations of Somatic Experiencing and its three-phase trauma resolution process. These chapters serve as a road map for both therapists and people, stressing the necessity of providing a safe atmosphere for recovery and leading readers through each stage of the therapeutic journey.

Chapter 5 covers practical tools and practices for increasing bodily awareness, regulating stress, and recording sensations and emotions. Chapter 6 delves more into the significance of working with the body in trauma treatment, including ways for releasing stored energy and fostering relaxation.

What distinguishes this book is the real-life case studies offered in Chapter 7, which provide fascinating insights into the use of Somatic Experiencing in therapeutic practice. These examples not only demonstrate the efficacy of the treatment but also give essential insights and takeaways for both therapists and clients.

Furthermore, Chapters 8 and 9 discuss cultural factors and ethical requirements, highlighting the significance of cultural sensitivity and professional ethics in treatment. Finally, Chapter 10 investigates the incorporation of Somatic Experiencing into other modalities and describes the future directions of this revolutionary approach to healing.

In essence, "Somatic Experiencing Therapy" is an invaluable resource for anybody seeking trauma resolution and holistic healing. Whether you're a therapist looking to improve your practice or an individual seeking personal development, this book will offer you the information, skills, and inspiration you need to negotiate the complexity of trauma and promote meaningful healing.

CHAPTER ONE

Introduction To Somatic Experiencing

What Is Somatic Experiencing Therapy?

Somatic Experiencing treatment (SET) is a kind of treatment that focuses on resolving and healing trauma via focused attention to bodily feelings and physical experiences. Unlike standard talk therapy linguistic, which focuses largely on the cognitive and parts of the brain, SET recognizes that trauma is both a psychological and a physiological problem. It was created by Dr. Peter A. Levine, a pioneering figure in trauma treatment who realized the necessity of treating trauma on a physical level.

Therapists use SET to help people reconnect with their physical feelings and instincts, helping them to process and release the pent-up energy and tension caused by traumatic events.

This method enables people to manage their nervous system reactions and achieve a feeling of safety and control in the current moment.

Understanding The Mind-Body Connection

Understanding the mind-body link is at the heart of Somatic Experiencing Therapy. This notion acknowledges that our thoughts, emotions, and physiological experiences are inextricably linked and impact one another in fundamental ways. When a person is subjected to trauma, whether it is a single occurrence or sustained stress, the body's natural reaction is to activate the fight, flight, or freeze response.

However, if the trauma is severe or unresolved, the body may get locked in a state of hyperarousal or hyperarousal, resulting in a variety of physical and psychological symptoms. These symptoms might include anxiety, despair, chronic pain, digestive difficulties, and even autoimmune illnesses. Somatic Experiencing Therapy seeks to restore balance and harmony to an individual's system by treating trauma through the lens of the mind-body connection.

Brief History And Development Of Somatic Experiencing

The origins of Somatic Experiencing Therapy may be traced back to Dr. Peter A. Levine's studies of how animals in the wild recover from life-threatening circumstances without experiencing trauma. Levine's study revealed that animals had natural systems for releasing energy gathered during stressful situations, therefore delaying the formation of trauma-related illnesses.

Inspired by these discoveries, Levine sought to apply similar ideas to his work with human clients, resulting in the creation of Somatic Experiencing Therapy in the 1970s. Over time, SET has acquired recognition and acceptance in the area of trauma treatment, with multiple studies demonstrating its efficacy in treating PTSD, anxiety disorders, and other trauma-related diseases.

Somatic Experiencing Therapy is now performed internationally by qualified therapists who have undergone extensive training to grasp the ideas and procedures of this approach. Its holistic and body-centered approach to trauma recovery continues to provide hope and healing to those suffering from the aftereffects of previous traumatic events.

CHAPTER TWO

The Physiology Of Trauma

Exploring How Trauma Affects The Body

Trauma, whether it be a catastrophic accident, a lengthy period of stress, or a highly unpleasant incident, affects not just our emotions and thoughts, but also our physical bodies. Understanding how trauma affects the body is critical for comprehending the full spectrum of its effects and developing successful treatment techniques like Somatic Experiencing Therapy.

Trauma initiates a series of physiological reactions in the body, activating the sympathetic nervous system, sometimes known as the "fight or flight" response. This is an evolutionary reaction, intended to prepare us to cope with urgent challenges. However, with trauma, this response may become dysregulated, resulting in persistent activation and hyperarousal. This implies that even after the traumatic experience has gone, the body is still on high alert, ready to respond to imagined dangers. This persistent condition of hyperarousal may cause a variety of physical symptoms, including elevated heart rate, shallow breathing, muscular tension, and digestive problems.

Furthermore, trauma may affect the body's stress response system, including the hypothalamic-pituitary-adrenal (HPA) axis, which governs the synthesis of stress hormones such as cortisol. In circumstances of trauma, this system may become dysregulated, resulting in hyper- or hypo-activation of stress responses. This dysregulation may lead to a variety of physical and mental health issues, such as anxiety, sadness, and chronic pain.

Neurobiological Processes Involved In Trauma

To understand how trauma affects the body, it's necessary to investigate the neurological mechanisms at work. The brain is responsible for absorbing and reacting to traumatic situations. When we experience a traumatic incident, the amygdala, also known as the brain's "fear center," becomes hyperactive, activating the sympathetic nervous system and causing the production of stress chemicals.

Furthermore, trauma may cause changes in brain structure and function, especially in areas related to emotional regulation and danger detection, such as the amygdala, prefrontal cortex, and hippocampus. These alterations may include increased emotional reactivity, difficulty controlling emotions, and decreased memory processing, which are all classic symptoms of post-traumatic stress disorder (PTSD).

Furthermore, trauma may impair the body's capacity to regulate arousal levels, causing changes in sleep, appetite, and energy. These disturbances may increase the physiological and psychological symptoms of trauma, resulting in a vicious cycle of discomfort and dysregulation.

Impact Of Trauma On The Nervous System

Trauma has a significant influence on the neurological system, especially the autonomic nervous system (ANS), which controls involuntary basic activities including heart rate, digestion, and respiration. When confronted with a stressful incident, the ANS reacts by activating the sympathetic nervous system, preparing the body to act. This activation causes physiological changes that enhance survival, such as higher heart rate, dilated pupils, and greater attentiveness.

However, trauma may cause dysregulation of the ANS, leading it to get locked in hyperarousal or hyperarousal. In situations of hyperarousal, the sympathetic nervous system is persistently active, causing chronic tension and worry. In contrast, during hyperarousal, the parasympathetic nervous system, which is responsible for relaxation and restorative processes, may take over, resulting in feelings of numbness, detachment, and separation from oneself and the surroundings.

Furthermore, trauma may affect the vagus nerve, which is a major component of the parasympathetic nervous system that controls social interaction and the body's relaxation response. Dysregulation of the vagus nerve may cause difficulty building and sustaining relationships, as well as issues with emotional regulation and self-soothing.

Understanding the physiological effects of trauma on the body and nervous system is critical for creating effective therapies to assist people in their recovery process. Approaches like Somatic Experiencing Therapy, which addresses both the psychological and physiological elements of trauma, may help people regain balance in their bodies and brains, supporting healing and resilience.

CHAPTER THREE

Principles Of Somatic Experiencing

Core Principles And Concepts Of Somatic Experiencing

Somatic Experiencing (SE) is a therapy technique that focuses on the body's feelings and reactions to help with trauma recovery. SE is based on the notion that trauma is more than simply a cerebral or emotional event; it is profoundly embedded in the body. SE assists persons in processing and releasing accumulated traumatic energy by addressing body experiences and reactions.

One key premise of Somatic Experiencing is that the body seeks balance and healing on its own. When confronted with overwhelming events such as trauma, the body's normal self-regulating processes might be interrupted, resulting in symptoms such as anxiety, hypervigilance, or dissociation. SE helps the body complete its innate reactions to stressful situations, restoring balance and well-being.

Another important idea in Somatic Experiencing is "titration." This phrase refers to the gentle and progressive approach employed in treatment to prevent overpowering the nervous system. Instead of going directly into the most intense portions of a traumatic experience, SE therapists guide clients through little, digestible chunks at a time. Individuals may safely confront their experience without retraumatizing themselves by titrating the therapy process.

SE also stresses the necessity of monitoring physiological feelings and identifying changes in the neurological system. Clients have heightened awareness of physiological sensations, allowing them to notice when they are becoming dysregulated and use self-regulation procedures to return to homeostasis. This emphasis on body awareness enables patients to improve their resilience and self-regulation abilities outside of treatment sessions.

The Role Of The Therapist In Facilitating Healing

The therapist is an important part of Somatic Experiencing because they guide clients through the trauma recovery process. Unlike standard talk therapy, which focuses mostly on verbal communication, SE therapists pay special attention to the client's physical clues and nonverbal signs. Therapists provide a safe environment for clients to explore their somatic sensations without judgment or pressure by maintaining an attentive presence and empathetic listening.

The therapist must cultivate a caring and non-intrusive posture. Rather than leading the treatment process, SE therapists serve as supporting guides on the client's path to recovery. They provide gentle instruction and encouragement while enabling the client to explore their inner experiences at their speed.

Furthermore, SE therapists are trained to spot indicators of nervous system dysfunction and respond accordingly. Therapists assist clients control their arousal levels and handle overpowering feelings, creating a sense of safety and confinement within the therapeutic connection. This attentive control promotes the progressive release and resolution of traumatic energy held in the body.

Furthermore, Somatic Experiencing therapists are acutely aware of their physical feelings and reactions during sessions.

Therapists who are aware of their bodily sensations may better sympathize with clients and model good self-regulation skills. This physical presence develops a stronger connection and trust between the therapist and the client, which benefits the therapeutic process.

Creating A Safe Environment For Trauma Resolution

Creating a safe atmosphere is essential in Somatic Experiencing treatment because it helps clients examine their experience without being retraumatized or overwhelmed. Safety includes both physical and emotional components, ensuring that the therapeutic environment is free of any risks or triggers that might disrupt the client's nervous system.

Therapists start by creating clear boundaries and ground rules for the treatment process, including what clients may anticipate and how confidentiality will be maintained. This fosters a feeling of regularity and control, which is critical for those who have suffered trauma. Additionally, therapists promote open communication and cooperation, allowing clients to express their wants and preferences throughout the therapy process.

Furthermore, developing safety in SE entails cultivating a feeling of trust and attunement in the therapeutic interaction. Therapists provide empathy, respect, and acceptance to their clients, validating their experiences without judgment. Therapists help clients feel seen, heard, and understood by cultivating an environment of unconditional positive regard, which is critical for recovery.

Furthermore, therapists who use Somatic Experiencing encourage the progressive and careful examination of painful experiences, ensuring that clients are neither overwhelmed nor retraumatized throughout the process. Therapists use titration and pacing approaches to help clients go through the therapeutic journey at a tolerable pace, allowing for the progressive release and resolution of traumatic energy stored in the body.

Providing a safe environment for trauma resolution in Somatic experiences entails setting clear boundaries, cultivating trust and attunement, and pacing the therapy process in a manner that respects the client's nervous system. Clients who cultivate safety may embark on their recovery path with increased resilience, empowerment, and hope for the future.

CHAPTER FOUR

The Three-Phase Approach

Overview Of The Three Phases Of Somatic Experiencing Therapy

Somatic Experiencing Therapy (SET) is an effective therapy approach that addresses trauma and its consequences on the body and mind. At its foundation, SET is based on the idea that traumatic events may get imprisoned inside the body, resulting in a variety of physical and psychological symptoms. The three-phase method in SET provides a systematic framework for therapists and clients to efficiently traverse the healing process.

Phase 1: Establishing Safety And Stability

The initial phase of SET focuses on giving the customer a feeling of safety and stability. Trauma may damage a person's sense of safety in the environment, making them feel continually on edge or vulnerable. As a result, the therapist collaborates with the client to establish a secure environment in which they may explore their emotions without feeling overwhelmed.

During this phase, the therapist may use grounding methods to assist the client control their nervous system and be present in the moment. These strategies might include deep breathing exercises, mindfulness activities, or physical motions that increase body awareness.

Furthermore, the therapist and client collaborate to uncover the client's particular resources and qualities, which may help them through the recovery process. These resources might be internal (resilience or coping skills) or external (supporting relationships or hobbies).

Phase 2: Exploring The Trauma Narrative

Once safety and stability have been restored, the attention changes to investigating the trauma story. This phase entails carefully reliving the traumatic incident or events in a manner that helps the client to process and integrate their experiences without feeling overwhelmed.

The therapist leads the client through this process, urging them to notice sensations, feelings, and ideas that come as they recollect the event. Rather than re-traumatizing the client, the objective is to assist them gain a feeling of mastery and control over their interior experiences.

The therapist uses strategies like titration and pendulation to assist the client manage their arousal levels, ensuring that they stay within their "window of tolerance" where healing may occur. To avoid overload, this method may entail progressively approaching and then drawing back from distressing content.

Phase 3: Integration And Resolution

The third phase of SET is focused on integration and resolution, in which the client starts to make sense of their experiences and construct a cohesive narrative of their life story. This phase is distinguished by a growing feeling of self-awareness and empowerment as the client learns to connect to their trauma in novel ways.

Integration might include bringing new ideas and views obtained throughout the therapy process into the client's everyday life. This might involve adopting better-coping techniques, establishing boundaries, or creating a stronger sense of self-compassion.

Resolution does not imply that the trauma is completely erased or forgotten, but rather that its influence is greatly decreased, enabling the client to live more fully in the present now. It is a progressive and continual process that continues after official treatment is completed.

Somatic Experiencing Therapy's three-phase method provides an organized and comprehensive road to trauma recovery, enabling clients to reclaim their lives and move on with increased resilience and energy.

CHAPTER FIVE

Techniques And Tools

Body Awareness Exercises

Body awareness exercises are basic techniques used in Somatic Experiencing Therapy to help people reconnect with their physical feelings and experiences. These exercises attempt to increase awareness of physiological sensations, which are typically ignored or repressed, particularly during times of stress or trauma. Paying attention to body sensations may help clients reestablish a feeling of safety and control over their bodies.

One frequent body awareness exercise is just focusing attention on various regions of the body, beginning with the toes and gradually progressing upward to the head. Clients may be directed to observe any feelings, such as warmth, tingling, tension, or relaxation, in each section of the body as they concentrate their attention there. This practice promotes attention and presence in the body, resulting in a greater connection with oneself.

Mindful breathing is another helpful technique for increasing body awareness. Clients are urged to concentrate on the sensations of breathing, such as the rise and fall of the chest or the sensation of air going through the nose. Individuals may relax their nervous systems and center themselves in the present moment by focusing their attention on their breathing. This practice may be very useful for reducing anxiety and increasing relaxation.

Furthermore, body scanning is a common method utilized in body awareness exercises. Clients are instructed to scan their bodies from head to toe, paying special attention to any points of tension, pain, or relaxation. This technique helps people become more aware of their physiological feelings, which might indicate areas of buried stress or unresolved trauma. Clients may learn to relieve stress and better control their nervous systems by scanning their bodies regularly.

Overall, body awareness activities are crucial in Somatic Experiencing Therapy for increasing self-awareness, relaxation, and healing. Individuals who pay attention to their physiological feelings may get a better awareness of themselves and their experiences, opening the path for increased resilience and well-being.

Grounding Techniques For Managing Distress

Grounding strategies are very useful tools in Somatic Experiencing Therapy for reducing discomfort and restoring a feeling of safety and stability. When people are overwhelmed by emotions or feelings, grounding practices may help them return to the present moment and anchor them in their bodies. These strategies are particularly beneficial for those who have been traumatized or who are dealing with anxiety or dissociation.

One successful grounding approach is using the senses to link with the outside world. Clients may be instructed to observe five visible items, four tactile things, three auditory things, two olfactory things, and one gustatory thing. Individuals may anchor themselves in the current world by concentrating their attention on sensory experiences rather than unwanted ideas or overpowering emotions.

Another effective grounding strategy is to employ grounding items or anchors. Clients are urged to choose an item that has personal meaning or gives comfort, such as a cherished image, a smooth stone, or a piece of jewelry. When feeling overwhelmed, people might hold or concentrate on their grounding item to help them manage their emotions and be present in the moment.

Furthermore, grounding methods often include bodily sensations, such as deep breathing or gradual muscular relaxation. Clients may be instructed to take slow, deep breaths, concentrating on the feeling of air entering and exiting their bodies. Alternatively, they might tighten and then relax certain muscle groups to relieve stress and encourage relaxation.

Overall, grounding strategies are effective tools for reducing distress and enhancing emotional control in Somatic Experiencing Therapy. Individuals who incorporate these practices into their everyday lives may develop a stronger feeling of resilience and well-being, even in the face of adversity.

Tracking Sensations And Emotions

Tracking sensations and feelings is a key component of Somatic Experiencing Therapy, helping people to become more aware of their physical experiences and emotional states. During this process, clients are advised to pay attention to small shifts and changes in their bodies and emotions, which may provide vital information about their interior moods and underlying activation patterns.

A bodily sensation scale is one method for keeping track of feelings and emotions. Clients may be asked to assess the severity of different body sensations on a scale of 0 to 10, where 0 represents no experience and 10 represents severe pain or distress. Individuals who routinely monitor feelings in this manner might develop insight into how their bodies react to various stimuli and learn to recognize early warning signals of discomfort.

Journaling is another good way to keep track of feelings and emotions. Clients are invited to maintain a diary in which they may write their experiences, including anybody sensations, emotions, or ideas that occur throughout the day. Individuals who write regularly may see patterns and trends in their experiences, resulting in a better knowledge of their mental and physical well-being.

In addition to recording sensations, it is critical to pay attention to emotions and how the body reacts to them. Clients may be led to observe how emotions appear in their bodies, such as stiffness in the shoulders when nervous or a sinking sensation in the stomach when sad. Individuals who monitor their physiological reactions might learn to better manage their emotions and keep them from becoming overpowering.

Overall, monitoring sensations and emotions is an important activity in Somatic Experiencing Therapy for increasing self-awareness and emotional control. Individuals who cultivate a better knowledge of their physiological sensations might build more resilience and well-being in the face of life's obstacles.

Titration And Pendulation

Titration and pendulation are advanced strategies in Somatic Experiencing Therapy that assist people manage their arousal levels and safely process traumatic events. These strategies entail breaking down overpowering feelings or emotions into smaller, more manageable chunks, enabling clients to work through them gradually without being retraumatized.

Titration includes timing the treatment process so that clients are exposed to uncomfortable sensations or emotions in tiny, manageable amounts. Rather than rushing headlong into overpowering situations, clients are advised to approach them gently, pausing as required to manage their arousal levels and avoid overload. This sustained exposure helps people to develop resilience and tolerance to upsetting stimuli over time without being overwhelmed or retraumatized.

Pendulation, on the other hand, entails switching attention between feelings of safety and discomfort. Clients are taught to recognize periods of relaxation or peace in their bodies, even in the middle of upsetting circumstances. Individuals may better control their nervous systems and avoid overload by alternating between experiences of safety and anguish. This strategy helps clients develop resilience and distress tolerance, which aids in the processing of traumatic situations.

In Somatic Experiencing Therapy, titration and pendulation work together to give an organized approach to trauma processing and arousal level regulation. Individuals may safely work through trauma by dividing it down into smaller, more manageable portions and alternating between safety and anguish.

CHAPTER SIX

Working With The Body

Understanding Somatic Symptoms And Their Significance

Somatic experiencing therapy explores the complex relationship between the mind and body, recognizing that emotional experiences may appear physically. Somatic symptoms are physical feelings or experiences that stem from unresolved trauma or stress. They may include muscular tension, headaches, stomachaches, and shortness of breath. These signs are the body's method of indicating that something is wrong and needs attention.

Understanding these symptoms is critical in somatic experience treatment because they provide vital insights into the underlying difficulties.

For example, persistent stomachaches might suggest unresolved worry or dread, but chronic shoulder strain could indicate a history of trauma. Paying attention to these physical cues allows people to acquire insight into their emotional states and begin the healing process.

Identifying And Releasing Trapped Energy In The Body

Trapped energy refers to the emotional or physiological energy that remains in the body after a traumatic event. This energy may persist for years, causing tension, pain, and discomfort. Somatic experience therapy seeks to discover and release this stored energy, restoring the body to a state of balance and relaxation.

Pendulation is a method used in somatic experience therapy to alleviate stored energy. This entails carefully changing the emphasis from feelings of tension or pain to sensations of relaxation or ease. Individuals who oscillate between these opposing perceptions might eventually release imprisoned energy and regain a sense of balance.

Grounding exercises are another way to release imprisoned energy. These exercises entail connecting with the present moment and physical sensations of the body, such as feeling the feet on the ground or recognizing one's breath. Individuals may escape the hold of previous traumas by anchoring themselves in the present moment, allowing their bodies to relax and let go.

Techniques For Releasing Muscular Tension And Promoting Relaxation

Muscular tension is a frequent symptom of stress and trauma when the body braces itself in reaction to imagined dangers. Somatic experience therapy provides a variety of strategies for relieving muscle tension and encouraging relaxation, helping people to unwind and get relief from physical pain.

Progressive muscle relaxation is one such approach, in which various muscle groups in the body are progressively tensed and then relaxed in turn. Individuals who deliberately contract and release muscles might become more aware of regions of tension and learn to let go of stress contained in the body.

Breathing exercises are another effective method of achieving calm. Deep, diaphragmatic breathing may stimulate the body's relaxation response, which counteracts the effects of the stress reaction. Slow, regular breathing may help people quiet their nervous systems and generate a sensation of relaxation and peace.

Body awareness is central to somatic experience treatment. Individuals may have a better awareness of themselves and their experiences by tuning in to their bodies feelings and learning to listen to their cues. Pendulation, grounding exercises, gradual muscle relaxation, and breathing exercises may all help to release stored energy, relieve physical tension, and promote relaxation, opening the path for healing and development.

CHAPTER SEVEN

Titration And Pendulation

Understanding The Concept Of Titration

Titration is a core element of Somatic Experiencing Therapy, typically compared to carefully adjusting a dimmer switch rather than turning a light on and off. It entails breaking down daunting situations into smaller, more manageable chunks. Imagine you're dealing with a massive, chaotic flood of emotions and feelings. Instead of rushing headlong into the furious torrent, titration recommends putting your toes in first and gradually acclimatizing to the water's warmth and speed.

In therapy, titration refers to encountering upsetting information in modest, manageable amounts. It's about striking the perfect balance between expressing unpleasant emotions and being safe and grounded throughout the process. Individuals who pace their trauma inquiry might avoid getting overwhelmed or re-traumatized by their experiences.

During titration, the therapist takes the subject through modest stages, enabling them to recognize sensations, emotions, and ideas without feeling overwhelmed. This process permits the nervous system to progressively adapt to the activation brought on by traumatic memories or events. Titration, like the slow stretching of a muscle to avoid damage, aids the nervous system's adaptation without creating more suffering.

Practicing Pendulation Between Sensations Of Safety And Discomfort

Pendulation is another important notion in Somatic Experiencing Therapy, which is closely connected to titration.

It includes a cyclic oscillation between feelings of safety and discomfort, similar to the ebb and flow of ocean waves. Imagine yourself standing on the beach, feeling the warm sand under your feet one minute and the chilly water the next.

In therapy, pendulation assists people in transitioning between states of calm and distress. It's a dynamic procedure in which the therapist encourages the client to experience both sensations of safety and discomfort, helping them to build resilience and efficiently manage their nervous system reactions.

During pendulation, the therapist may instruct the client to notice moments of comfort and relaxation in their body, such as the gradual rise and fall of their breath or the warmth of their palms. These feelings act as anchors, keeping the person in the present moment and offering a sense of safety in the face of distress.

Pendulation also entails carefully transferring the focus from regions of tension or pain to areas of relaxation. Individuals who alternate between these opposing experiences might learn to bear uncomfortable feelings while establishing a sense of balance and stability within themselves.

Gradual Exposure To Traumatic Material

Gradual exposure is an important component of Somatic Experiencing Therapy because it allows people to handle distressing information at a pace that is comfortable for them. Rather than plunging headfirst into the depths of their trauma, gradual exposure takes little, incremental effort to explore painful memories or feelings.

In therapy, the therapist works with the client to provide a secure and supportive setting for discussing traumatic experiences. They may begin by gradually introducing components of the trauma story or concentrating on particular feelings linked with the traumatic event.

As the individual's comfort and confidence in their capacity to endure painful information grows, the therapist steadily raises the intensity and complexity of exposure exercises. This might include reviewing unpleasant memories in more detail or confronting difficult emotions that develop throughout the process.

Throughout the progressive exposure phase, the therapist attentively watches the client's reactions to ensure that they feel supported and empowered to navigate their emotional environment. By tackling trauma in a methodical and controlled way, people may progressively integrate traumatic events into their larger sense of self, supporting healing and resilience over time.

CHAPTER EIGHT

Cultural Considerations

Addressing Diversity And Cultural Sensitivity In Somatic Experiencing Therapy

Diversity and cultural awareness are critical in Somatic Experiencing Therapy (SET). Every person comes from a distinct cultural background, influenced by traditions, beliefs, and experiences that form their worldview and reactions to trauma. To offer effective and inclusive treatment, therapists must first identify and appreciate these distinctions.

Understanding how trauma expresses itself differently among cultures is a critical component of tackling diversity in SET. What is considered traumatic in one culture may not be so in another. For example, an automobile accident may cause significant anguish in someone from a Western society, but it may not have the same impact on someone from a country where fatal accidents are regrettably more prevalent. Therapists must approach each client with cultural humility, acknowledging that their interpretation of trauma may vary from their own.

Furthermore, cultural sensitivity in SET entails understanding and upholding cultural norms and values. Therapists must get acquainted with their clients' cultural origins to prevent unintentionally imposing their cultural prejudices on the therapy process. This entails being willing to learn about other cultural traditions, beliefs, and communication styles. Direct eye contact, for example, may be considered rude in certain cultures but a sign of interest and concentration in others. By being aware of these subtleties, therapists may provide a secure and supportive atmosphere in which clients feel understood and welcomed.

Recognizing the effect of systemic injustice and intergenerational trauma on disadvantaged populations is an important component of addressing diversity in SET. Historical injustices, discrimination, and societal inequities may have a substantial impact on a person's trauma experience as well as their capacity to receive and participate in treatment. Therapists must be aware of these larger cultural variables and collaborate with clients to negotiate their impact on mental health and well-being.

Adapting Techniques For Different Cultural Contexts

Flexibility is essential in Somatic Experiencing Therapy when it comes to adapting procedures to various cultural situations. While the underlying concepts of SET are similar, how they are applied may differ depending on cultural conventions, beliefs, and preferences. Therapists must be prepared to adapt their technique to fit each client's specific requirements, taking into consideration their cultural background and worldview.

One method for adapting approaches in SET is to include culturally appropriate metaphors and symbols in the therapy process. Metaphors are effective in expressing complicated concepts and emotions, and employing culturally appropriate metaphors may assist bridge the gap between the therapist and the client. For example, in certain indigenous societies, the "medicine wheel" represents balance and connectivity. Integrating such symbols into therapy discussions might help the client feel more connected and empowered.

Furthermore, therapists may use traditional healing traditions and rituals from the client's culture to supplement SET procedures. Many cultures have strong healing traditions that highlight the mind-body link and the value of group support. Integrating components of these traditions into therapy allows therapists to draw into the client's existing resources and resilience, generating a deeper feeling of healing and integration.

When dealing with clients from various cultural backgrounds, therapists must also consider language difficulties and communication methods. Language is more than simply a means of communication; it also conveys cultural meanings and subtleties. Therapists should use straightforward and basic language, avoiding jargon or idioms that the client may not understand. Furthermore, hiring translators or multilingual therapists may assist in guaranteeing that the client understands and actively participates in the therapy process.

Challenges And Opportunities In Cross-Cultural Therapy

Cross-cultural treatment in Somatic Experiencing offers both obstacles and opportunities for therapists. On the one hand, overcoming cultural differences and misconceptions may be difficult and needs continuous reflection and change. Therapists must approach cross-cultural therapy with humility and openness, acknowledging that they may not always have all the answers and that learning from their clients' cultural viewpoints is an important part of the therapeutic process.

One of the most significant obstacles in cross-cultural therapy is the potential for cultural appropriation or insensitivity. Therapists must be aware of their cultural prejudices and refrain from forcing their ideas or opinions on their clients. This necessitates a willingness to engage in self-reflection and cultural competency training to better comprehend the dynamics of power and privilege in the therapeutic interaction.

However, cross-cultural therapy provides unique chances for development and learning. Therapists may broaden their knowledge of trauma and resilience by working with clients from other cultural backgrounds, allowing them to create more inclusive and successful therapeutic techniques. Building cultural competency not only improves therapists' capacity to interact with various clients, but also enriches their personal and professional life by instilling more empathy, humility, and respect for cultural differences.

Furthermore, cross-cultural therapy may spur societal change by questioning prevailing narratives and encouraging cultural humility and understanding. Therapists may help to demolish systematic oppression and build a more fair and equitable society by providing clients with safe and inclusive settings in which to explore their cultural identities and experiences.

To summarize, addressing diversity and cultural sensitivity in Somatic Experiencing Therapy requires therapists to approach each client with humility, openness, and respect for their cultural background and experiences. By adapting procedures to varied cultural settings, therapists may create a more inclusive and successful therapy environment that values each individual's unique strengths and resilience. While cross-cultural therapy has its obstacles, it also provides important chances for personal development, learning, and societal change.

CHAPTER NINE

Ethical And Professional Guidelines

Code Of Ethics For Somatic Experiencing Practitioners

Adherence to a strong code of ethics is essential in Somatic Experiencing Therapy. It acts as a guiding light, ensuring that practitioners maintain the greatest levels of professionalism, honesty, and client care. This code serves as a model for ethical behavior, describing the essential concepts and obligations that practitioners must follow in their work.

Commitment to customer welfare is one of the code of ethics guiding principles. Practitioners agree to put their customers' well-being and safety above everything else. This entails creating a safe, respectful, and nonjudgmental atmosphere in which clients feel empowered to freely explore their inner experiences. Furthermore, practitioners must ensure that their interventions are always in the client's best interests, avoiding any activities that might result in injury or exploitation.

Integrity and honesty are also important components of the code of ethics. Practitioners are required to uphold the highest standards of ethics in all dealings with customers, coworkers, and the larger community. This involves being open about their credentials, experience, and limits as practitioners. Furthermore, practitioners must behave themselves ethically in financial affairs, ensuring that their fees are appropriate and free of conflicts of interest.

Confidentiality is a fundamental trust in Somatic Experiencing Therapy. Practitioners must maintain the privacy and confidentiality of their client's information at all times. This includes using caution when discussing cases with colleagues, seeking informed permission before disclosing any client information, and implementing proper security measures to protect sensitive data. by adhering to rigorous confidentiality requirements, practitioners establish a secure environment in which clients may discuss their most sensitive experiences without fear of criticism or exposure.

Cultural competency and diversity are also important components of the code of ethics. Practitioners must acknowledge and respect their clients' cultural, ethnic, and socioeconomic variety, tailoring their therapeutic approach to each individual's specific needs and preferences. This necessitates constant education and self-reflection to recognize and address any biases or preconceptions that may exist in the therapeutic interaction. By embracing diversity, practitioners may provide an open and inviting workplace in which all clients feel valued and understood.

Finally, the code of ethics stresses the need for professional limits. To ensure the therapy relationship's integrity and efficacy, practitioners must set clear and acceptable boundaries with their clients. This involves presenting a professional image, avoiding parallel relationships, and abstaining from any sort of exploitation or abuse. Setting and maintaining clear boundaries allows practitioners to develop a framework that supports the therapeutic process while also guaranteeing their own and their client's safety and well-being.

In conclusion, the code of ethics for Somatic Experiencing practitioners provides a foundation for ethical behavior in the area of treatment. By adhering to these values, practitioners maintain the greatest levels of professionalism, honesty, and client care, fostering a safe and supportive atmosphere for healing to occur.

Maintaining Boundaries And Confidentiality

It is critical to preserve boundaries and secrecy while doing Somatic Experiencing Therapy. Boundaries serve as the structure for the therapeutic interaction, providing clarity, safety, and respect for both the practitioner and the client. Confidentiality, on the other hand, is the foundation of trust, giving customers the comfort that their most private ideas and experiences will be kept safe and secure.

Setting and maintaining boundaries starts with the initial encounter between practitioner and client. Practitioners must properly describe the boundaries of the therapeutic relationship, including both participants' duties and obligations, the scope of the treatment, and any constraints that may apply. This establishes the foundation for a collaborative and respectful collaboration in which both the practitioner and the client understand and agree on the parameters of involvement.

Within the therapeutic environment, boundaries serve many purposes. They define the physical, emotional, and psychological boundaries between the practitioner and the client, ensuring that both parties retain a feeling of autonomy and agency. Practitioners must be cognizant of proper bodily boundaries and avoid any acts or gestures that might be seen as invasive or boundary-violating. Emotionally, boundaries govern the intensity and depth of the therapeutic interaction, preventing the practitioner from becoming too involved or enmeshed.

Confidentiality is a fundamental trust in Somatic Experiencing Therapy. Clients must be satisfied that their personal information and experiences will be kept secret, with only a few exceptions permitted by law or ethical norms. Before revealing any information, practitioners must get clients' informed permission, ensuring that clients understand the constraints of confidentiality and the situations under which disclosure may be required. Additionally, practitioners must make reasonable efforts to secure and maintain client records, whether in electronic or physical form, to prevent illegal access or disclosure.

Maintaining boundaries and confidentiality requires continual monitoring and self-awareness on behalf of the practitioner. It requires being able to understand and manage the complexities of the therapeutic relationship, as well as react flexibly and effectively to each client's changing needs and dynamics.

Practitioners must be aware of symptoms of boundary violations or breaches of confidentiality and address them swiftly and honestly to rebuild trust and preserve the therapy process' integrity.

In conclusion, respecting boundaries and secrecy is critical in Somatic Experiencing Therapy. Practitioners provide a secure and respectful atmosphere where healing may occur naturally, free of judgment or interference, by setting clear and appropriate boundaries and protecting the confidentiality of client information.

Professional Development And Ongoing Training

Professional growth and continued training are critical for Somatic Experiencing Therapy practitioners to keep current on the newest research, methodologies, and best practices. Continuous learning not only improves the practitioner's knowledge and abilities, but it also guarantees that they can give the best possible care to their customers by changing and growing in response to new insights and advancements in the area.

Professional development includes a wide variety of activities such as formal education, workshops, seminars, conferences, and self-directed study. Practitioners must actively seek out chances for learning and development, exploring areas of interest or expertise that are relevant to their professional objectives and the requirements of their customers. This might include taking part in advanced training programs, getting specialist certifications, or engaging in peer supervision and consultation to improve their knowledge and competency in certain areas of Somatic Experiencing Therapy.

Ongoing training is especially vital in a quickly growing area like Somatic Experiencing Therapy, where new research and approaches are continually being developed. Practitioners must keep up with the newest advancements in the profession, critically analyzing new material and incorporating it into their practice conscientiously and ethically. This may need a willingness to question established assumptions and views while being open-minded and interested as they pursue new routes of study and discovery.

Furthermore, professional development goes beyond clinical skills to include larger dimensions of professional practice including ethics, cultural competency, and self-care. Practitioners must have a thorough awareness of ethical concepts and rules, and use them deliberately and consistently in their dealings with clients and colleagues. They must also work to improve their cultural competency, understanding and appreciating the variety of human experiences and tailoring their approach to treatment appropriately. Furthermore, practitioners must emphasize self-care and well-being, understanding that their physical, emotional, and psychological health has a direct influence on their capacity to successfully assist and empower their clients.

In conclusion, professional growth and continued training are critical aspects of Somatic Experiencing Therapy practice. By committing to lifelong learning and development, practitioners guarantee that they can deliver the best care to their clients while always growing and adapting to meet the ever-changing requirements of the people they serve.

CHAPTER TEN

Integration And Beyond

Integrating Somatic Experiencing Into Other Therapeutic Modalities

Integrating Somatic Experiencing (SE) into other therapy modalities may significantly improve the efficacy of treatment for a variety of psychiatric problems. SE, which emphasizes the body's intrinsic potential to recover from trauma, may supplement and improve standard talk therapy techniques.

A comprehensive approach that blends SE aspects with approaches from cognitive-behavioral therapy (CBT), dialectical behavior therapy (DBT), or psychodynamic therapy is one method for integrating SE into other modalities. For example, in CBT, practitioners might use SE methods to assist clients become more aware of their physical sensations and how these connect to their thoughts and emotions. This may help the clients better understand themselves and how they respond to stimuli.

SE may be incorporated into DBT by teaching clients how to control their emotions and endure suffering. By concentrating on physical sensations and using SE treatments like as grounding methods or pendulation, clients may learn to be present with their emotions without getting overwhelmed.

Another approach is to include SE in trauma-focused treatments like Eye Movement Desensitization and Reprocessing (EMDR) or Sensorimotor Psychotherapy. SE may offer new tools and perspectives to traditional techniques, helping therapists deal more effectively with complicated trauma and somatic symptoms.

Overall, when integrating SE into other therapeutic modalities, therapists must have a good awareness of both SE concepts and the principles of the other modalities. Therapists may give their clients more complete and successful therapy by integrating the qualities of several techniques.

Continuing Personal And Professional Growth As A Therapist

Therapists who practice Somatic Experiencing Therapy (SET) or any other therapeutic modality must maintain ongoing personal and professional development. As therapists, our personal growth has a direct impact on our capacity to be present and sensitive to our clients, while continual professional development ensures that we are up to speed on the most recent research and approaches in the industry.

Therapists may continue their development via their therapeutic practice. Engaging in therapy helps us to address our unresolved problems and get a better understanding of how they could affect our work with clients. By understanding our tendencies and triggers, we may become more compassionate and effective therapists.

Therapists may also continue their development via activities like mindfulness, meditation, or yoga. These techniques may help us remain grounded and present at work, lowering burnout and enhancing our sensitivity and compassion.

On the professional front, therapists may advance their knowledge by attending seminars, conferences, and training in Somatic Experiencing and other pertinent modalities. These possibilities enable therapists to expand their knowledge of trauma and improve their professional abilities. Supervision and consultation with experienced clinicians give vital assistance and direction to therapists as they manage complicated situations.

Therapists may improve their efficacy and offer the greatest treatment for their clients by focusing on both personal and professional development.

The Future Of Somatic Experiencing Therapy And Its Potential Impact

Somatic Experiencing Therapy (SET) has the potential to broaden its reach and impact on individuals, communities, and even society as a whole. As people become more aware of the effects of trauma, SET has the potential to play an important role in addressing and healing trauma-related symptoms.

One direction for the future of SET is greater integration into settings other than traditional therapy offices.

This could include schools, hospitals, workplaces, and community centers. Bringing SET techniques into these settings allows more people to benefit from trauma-informed care and learn how to regulate their nervous systems in the face of stress and adversity.

Furthermore, ongoing research into the neurobiology of trauma and the efficacy of SET is likely to yield new insights and treatment strategies. This could lead to improvements to the SET model and the creation of new interventions to address specific types of trauma or populations with special needs.

Another consideration for the future of SET is its potential impact on social justice and collective healing. By addressing individual trauma, SET can contribute to larger movements for social change and healing. As more people become aware of their own somatic experiences and learn to regulate their nervous systems, they may become more empathetic, resilient, and capable of bringing about positive change in their communities.

Overall, the future of SET looks promising, with the potential to transform individual lives, strengthen communities, and contribute to a more compassionate and just society. As therapists and advocates continue to champion SET's principles, its impact will only grow and evolve in the coming years.

Conclusion

To summarize, Somatic Experiencing Therapy (SET) provides a comprehensive approach to trauma healing by combining physiological sensations, emotions, and cognitive processes. This treatment approach, established by Dr. Peter A. Levine, stresses the body's intrinsic potential to recover from traumatic events. Through gentle inquiry and understanding of physical sensations, SET tries to liberate stored energy linked with trauma, enabling people to renegotiate their connection with the traumatic experience.

The efficacy of SET depends on its capacity to treat both the physiological and psychological elements of trauma, offering a complete foundation for recovery. By assisting people to safely experience and manage physiological feelings connected with trauma, SET develops resilience and empowerment.

Furthermore, SET addresses the intricate connection between the mind and body, understanding that trauma is retained not just in memories but also in bodily sensations and nervous system reactions. By developing self-awareness and somatic mindfulness, SET helps people recover a feeling of control over their bodies and lives.

Overall, the concepts of Somatic Experiencing Therapy provide a potential path for trauma healing, especially for those who have struggled with standard talk treatments or who exhibit somatic symptoms connected to their trauma. As research continues to explore the efficacy of SET and its applications across diverse populations, it stands as a valuable resource in the field of trauma treatment, offering hope and healing to those in need.

THE END